BREAKFAST WITH THOM GUNN

PHOENIX POETS

BREAKFAST WITH THOM GUNN

RANDALL MANN

THE UNIVERSITY OF CHICAGO PRESS *Chicago and London*

RANDALL MANN is a writer and editor living in San Francisco. He is the author of a poetry book entitled *Complaint in the Garden*, winner of the 2003 *Kenyon Review* prize, and the coauthor of a textbook entitled *Writing Poems*.

The University of Chicago Press, Chicago 60637
The University of Chicago Press, Ltd., London
© 2009 by The University of Chicago
All rights reserved. Published 2009
Printed in the United States of America
18 17 16 15 14 13 12 11 10 09   1 2 3 4 5

ISBN-13: 978-0-226-50343-1 (cloth)
ISBN-13: 978-0-226-50344-8 (paper)
ISBN-10: 0-226-50343-7 (cloth)
ISBN-10: 0-226-50344-5 (paper)

Library of Congress Cataloging-in-Publication Data
Mann, Randall.
  Breakfast with Thom Gunn / Randall Mann.
  p. cm. — (Phoenix poets series)
  Poems.
  ISBN-13: 978-0-226-50343-1 (cloth : alk. paper)
  ISBN-13: 978-0-226-50344-8 (pbk. : alk. paper)
  ISBN-10: 0-226-50343-7 (cloth : alk. paper)
  ISBN-10: 0-226-50344-5 (pbk. : alk. paper)
  I. Title. II. Series: Phoenix poets.
PS3613.A55B74 2009
811'.6—dc22
                                2008039079

♾ The paper used in this publication meets the minimum requirements of the American National Standard for Information Sciences—Permanence of Paper for Printed Library Materials, ANSI Z39.48-1992.

*For George O. Kolombatovich
and Tom Halloran*

Contents

Acknowledgments · ix

I

Early Morning on Market Street · 3
Election Day · 4
But · 5
Politics · 6
Fetish · 8
Song · 9
Queen Christina · 11
The Mortician in San Francisco · 12
Aubade · 14
Bernal Hill · 15
The Sunset · 16
Abandoned Landscapes · 17
Short Short · 18
Charity · 19
Ruin · 20
Pure · 21
Last Call · 22

II

Pastoral · 27
Syntax · 28
Little Colonial Song · 29
The Lake of Nostalgia · 30

The End of Landscape · 31
Ode · 33
Night: A Fragment · 35
Breakfast with Thom Gunn · 36
Ovid in San Francisco · 37
Ganymede on Polk Street · 39
Orpheus at Café Flore · 40
Modern Art · 41
To Francis Bacon · 42
Stranded · 43
Reception · 44
Career · 45
Postcard from California · 46
The Long View · 47
N · 48

III

Ocean Beach · 51
Translation · 52
Lexington · 53
Design · 54
The Rape of Ganymede · 55
Colloquy between A and B · 56
Intimacy · 57
Monday · 58
Seeking · 59
Well, Here We Are · 60
A View · 61
South City · 62
Poetry · 63
Fiction · 64

Notes · 65

Acknowledgments

Grateful acknowledgment is made to the editors of the following publications, in which these poems, often in slightly different form, first appeared:

Bloom: "Modern Art" and "Pastoral"
Cimarron Review: "Politics"
Court Green: "Queen Christina"
Fourteen Hills: "Lexington"
Gulf Coast: "The Rape of Ganymede"
Literary Imagination: "Intimacy" and "Ocean Beach"
Lodestar Quarterly: "Fetish" and "Song"
MiPOesias: "A View"
Pleiades: "Little Colonial Song," "Stranded," "The Long View," and "The Sunset"
Poetry: "Bernal Hill," "Career," "Charity," "Early Morning on Market Street," "Last Call," "N," and "Pure"
Quarterly West: "Ode" (Issue #51)
Salmagundi: "Aubade," "But," "Ovid in San Francisco," and "The End of Landscape"
Spork: "Abandoned Landscapes," "Ganymede on Polk Street," "Orpheus at Café Flore," "Postcard from California," and "Short Short"
Subtropics: "Fiction" appeared as "Nonfiction;" "Monday;" "Poetry;" and "Translation"
Western Humanities Review: "The Mortician in San Francisco"

"Breakfast with Thom Gunn" was first published in *The Kenyon Review*, Summer 2006, vol. XXVII, no. 3.

"Election Day" was first published in *Mantis 4: Poetry and Politics*.
"Night: A Fragment" first appeared in *JAMA 283(4): 2000. Copyright © 2000, American Medical Association*. All rights reserved.
"Ruin" was first published in *The Paris Review* 163 (Fall 2002).
"The Sunset" was reprinted in *Verse Daily* on June 27, 2007.

Many thanks to Michelle Boisseau, Geoffrey Brock, William Logan, Wayne Miller, Aaron Smith, and Sidney Wade for their careful readings of these poems. And thank you to Randy Petilos for his belief in this book.

I

*Body my house
my horse my hound
what will I do
when you are fallen*

— MAY SWENSON, "QUESTION"

Early Morning on Market Street

The moon, once full, is snow.
The line of transplanted trees,
thin and bloodless. The pink neon
bakery sign, *Sweet Inspiration*,

a mockery of loneliness—
but no one cares to eat, we souls
of this hour jacked up on what-
ever. And though desire

is a dirty word these days, what
else to call the idling car, its passenger door
pushed open; or the shirtless man—
he must be mad, tweaked out on speed—

outside his door
at Beck's Motor Lodge, staring
for hunger or mercy. Or me,
rubbing dirt from my eyes, wanting,

again, a man I do not want.

Election Day

God isn't art, early in the century,
He's pragmatism. I need Him
in this little city by the sea.

The day does its melancholy thing.
I come home, watch pornography,
fast-forward the scenes in which a friend—

back in his methamphetamine years—
has unrepeatable things done to him.
On the street,

a bag of paranoia costs less
than a moderately priced meal out.
I'll stay in. Tired

of the age of irony, everything
a gesture; tired of the word *gesture*,
the day ends

as the world will end:
eleven o'clock news, our charmingly corrupt
mayor incredulous, and a beautiful shot

of uncounted ballots floating in the bay.

But

That's a divine conjunction,
shouts Reverend Fitch
at Glide Memorial. *But*
the Lord will not pass you by.

I walked to church
through the botched
landscape of the Tenderloin:
piss-in-the-sink hotels and Triple-X;

the drunk sipping devotedly
from a paper sack. I
am no different.
Sometimes, coming home

in the fading light,
I cruise the steps
atop Sanchez Street
for love,

the hills above
cleansed and durable and indifferent:
Pass me not, O gentle savior.
Do not pass me by.

Politics

This is what he dreams of:
a map of burned land,
a mound of dirt
in the early century's winter.

A map of burned land?
A country is razed
in the early century's winter.
And God descends.

A country is raised
because of industry.
And God descends,
messengers rush inside

because of industry,
in spite of diplomats.
Messengers rush inside
to haunt the darkened aisles.

In spite of diplomats,
the witnesses know well
to haunt the darkened aisles,
experimentally—

the witnesses know well
that ushers dressed in black
experimentally
lurk by the cushioned seats.

That ushers dress in black
should tell you something:
lurking by the cushioned seats,
the saved and the terrible.

I should tell you something:
this is what he dreams of,
the saved and the terrible—
a mound of dirt.

Fetish

1.

Another Saturday, and the straights
and amateurs will come to my ghetto tonight.
Suspension of rights for all, I say.

2.

The vernacular? Those who snort speed
are called *bag whores*; those who shoot
are said to *slam*. They'll be over shortly.

3.

Apply enough waterproof mascara, Tourmaline-
Charged Eye Cream; tweeze the brows—just so.
Beauty, our politics, is local.

4.

I know that love is more than leather,
a tight white shirt, a good stink—
tonight, I am a fetish. I am canonical.

Song

18th and Castro Streets—
the center of the world!
Our world. We sip our tea,
the two of us derailed...

Outside the Midnight Sun,
men smoke. And dish. Life's *hard*.
The tea is turning cold.
The men are getting tired.

"These queens," my friend Steve says.
"A bag of speed will buy
you almost anyone—
almost any boy."

I lure him to the house,
online, with crystal meth.
I say to bring his friends.
I say I'll fuck his mouth.

(One time, I swear to God,
I fucked for weeks and weeks.)
These queens arrive, all prim,
and talk about antiques

and art, boring stuff.
But when they snort the best
crystal money can buy?
They *beg* to sit on my fist.

Queen Christina

To celebrate his final Pride, in June,
my friend, lymphatic, thin, and in distress,
managed to dress in drag. He shot the moon:
outstretched, he'd used his dying to think—obsess—

about the Prada pumps, their skin a snake;
the heavy pantyhose, two pair; the moot
but lacy underthings; the makeup, cake,
to overlay his pain. I called him *beaut-*

i-ful; he said he felt like Greta Garbo
in *Queen Christina* (our campy interplay);
I countered that he looked more like a hobo-
sexual in heels. We howled. That day,

we never left his Castro flat. His rhinestone
glittered, and everywhere, the smell of cologne.

The Mortician in San Francisco

This may sound queer,
but in 1985 I held the delicate hands
of Dan White:
I prepared him for burial; by then, Harvey Milk
was made monument—no, myth—by the years
since he was shot.

I remember when Harvey was shot:
twenty, and I knew I was queer.
Those were the years,
Levi's and leather jackets holding hands
on Castro Street, cheering for Harvey Milk—
elected on the same day as Dan White.

I often wonder about Supervisor White,
who fatally shot
Mayor Moscone and Supervisor Milk,
who was one of us, a Castro queer.
May 21, 1979: a jury hands
down the sentence, seven years—

in truth, five years—
for ex-cop, ex-fireman Dan White,
for the blood on his hands;
when he confessed that he had shot
the mayor and the queer,
a few men in blue cheered. And Harvey Milk?

Why cry over spilled milk,
some wondered, semi-privately, for years—
it meant "one less queer."
The jurors turned to White.
If just the mayor had been shot,
Dan might have had trouble on his hands—

but the twelve who held his life in their hands
maybe didn't mind the death of Harvey Milk;
maybe, the second murder offered him a shot
at serving only a few years.
In the end, he committed suicide, this Dan White.
And he was made presentable by a queer.

Aubade

Those who lack a talent for love have come
to walk the long Pier 7. Here at the end
of the imagined world are three low-flying gulls

like lies on the surface; the slow red
of a pilot's boat; the groan
of a fisherman hacking a small shark—

and our speech like the icy water, a poor
translation that will not carry us across.
What brought us west, anyway? A hunger.

But ours is no Donner Party, we who feed
only on scenery, the safest form
of obfuscation: see how the bay is a gray

deepening into gray, the color of heartbreak.

Bernal Hill

Something has to give.
We stand above it all.
Below, the buildings' tall
but tiny narrative.

The water's always near,
you say. And so are you,
for now. It has to do.
There's little left to fear.

A wind so cold, one might
forget that winter's gone.
The city lights are on
for us, to us, tonight.

The Sunset

Fog, like reason, settles on the peeling district.
This is the new money. The new economy.
Where my lover lives. When I left him,
I left books, coats, silverware. Things.
It wasn't charity; it was an impure,
commonplace case of forgetting. (May he find some use

for my low-rent betrayals.) Land ends
with miles of aloe along the Great Highway.
Surfers strip off their suits, half-naked
to the naked sea. The sand's ignored
BEWARE OF THE UNDERTOW signs:
these are the notes of the drowned.

Abandoned Landscapes

1.

So Kansas City tucked its cock, spritzed its wig,
drove to the drag show at Missie B's.

2.

Night. A heater groused, a fan belted out. Oh—
and there was fever and there was rash.

3.

In the john, I focused heroically on the urinal cake; I tried
to flush without flourish. But my gestures betrayed me.

4.

I fell for the Seville-style tile of the Plaza, the oldest
strip-mall on the continent. Commerce was history.

5.

Fuck it. Let's smoke a pack of cloves and play
the Decemberists—*Picaresque*, perhaps—one last time.

Short Short

Hard maples, then.
A murder of crows.
This is the Missouri of my life—

almost. Everything's almost:
sky, fountain, parkway.
I am a literal _____.

Imagine this: late solipsism,
the positive blood test, the end
of words. The end.

Charity

Starlings' racket; the staining redbud. The, a, day. I fall
apart from myself—there is no one else. Charity
sounds like the water-pump in the wall; my vanity,
a tiny city of salves, acids and all,
steep bottles with hopeful names. I am,
inside. Time for the words *mask*, *ritual*, and *exam*.

Ruin

Already Judah Street awaits the rain
of streetcar-whine down avenues of rain—
the snap of black umbrellas, the falling coin.
We strangers on the train ignore the rain,
observe two boys in neon slickers run
to catch their bus. Too late! Stuck in the rain,
the boy who's taller smacks the smaller one,
his passion given license by the rain.

I had a birthday yesterday. It's mine:
perversion, self-deceit, nostalgia, rain.
(My stop. I'll brush against a dozen men
before I disembark into the rain
an older, rumpled man. If life is ruin,
then let it burn like Rome, like Dante's rain.)

Pure

Purgatory must be like this,
myopic, wet, all noise white,
the ocean inexhaustible.

The old woman to our right
could have been a saint, clothed
in layers and layers of white.

And the terns, they strutted
then scattered when a sopping dog
ran in, then out, of the thick fog.

I was grateful you had pulled
me away from my dull schedule
for that walk, though I,

selfish to the end,
could not bring myself to say so.
I'll say it now, too late:

purgatory will be like this:
the nothingness behind us,
the nothingness ahead;

you and I, arm in arm—
two men holding each other.

Last Call

A giant bird-
of-paradise
has climbed the bar:
in this paradise

there are no flowers,
no flowers at all.
When Happy Hour
becomes Last Call—

Adam in drag
our royalty—
we buy her gin
for eternity

(an unseen deejay
scores the years
with pulsing music
of the spheres).

Now the queen has gone,
gone again
in search of love,
in search of sin.

It's closing time.
You were not at fault.
I drain my glass
and lick the salt.

II

*Here we go again, said Alcibiades; it's always
the same. When Socrates is around, no one else
can get a look-in with the attractive men.*

— *The Symposium,* TR. CHRISTOPHER GILL

Pastoral

My heart, my prison, lies
in a landlocked town,

in its queer patio-bar, Ambrosia,
the martinis stiff and dirty—

pollen sexing the air,
the smell of your hair, my fear.

Syntax

Those were the flannel days, after
the Gainesville slayings, before the state
turned permanent red, AIDS still a reason
to cash in your 401(k)—in other words,

the early nineties. Yikes. And I
was a raver in Florida—whistle, bad skin,
snazzy backpack. I learned that the rope
isn't velvet; there never was a rope,

just some feral queen at the door:
Miss Thing, there is no guest list tonight!
Once in, one ate, in designated order,
a few choice letters of the alphabet . . .

I took a choking drag of a clove.
The letters tasted bitter, like love.

Little Colonial Song

My escort here, a Seminole,
      proclaims his love of Spain:
a little silver crucifix
      dangles from his chain.

"The moss is Spanish moss!" he shouts.
      His name is Matador.
Just so, he's Christian, hard to nail
      but easy to adore.

We enter the savanna plain;
      mosquitoes persecute.
The shrill and tuneless sound of thrush
      reminds me of Beirut.

When night is falling on the state,
      we'll eat our fish and loaves
of Wonder Bread before we head
      toward dark, sequestered groves.

A vulture crouches on a pine
      like a desktop lamp.
It waits for us to sleep or leave
      our offal from the camp.

The Lake of Nostalgia

Lots of ibis; a little blue heron,
that lavender neck; the lake
named for Another Brit in Florida.

Look at the water, beautiful
and shallow, like a moral failure.
Look at the time! Its watch-spring

like the curled tongue of a butterfly.

The End of Landscape

There's a certain sadness to this body of water
adjacent to the runway, its reeds and weeds,
handful of ducks, the water color

manmade. A still life. And still
life's a cold exercise in looking back,
back to Florida, craning my neck

like a sandhill crane in Alachua Basin.
As for the scrub oaks,
the hot wind in the leaves *was* language,

Spanish moss—dusky, parasitic—
an obsession: I wanted to live in it.
(One professor in exile did,

covered himself in the stuff as a joke—
then spent a week removing mites.) That's
enough. The fields of rushes lay filled

with water, and I said farewell,
my high ship an old, red Volvo DL,
gone to another coast, another peninsula,

one without sleep or amphibious music.
Tonight, in flight from San Francisco—
because everything is truer at a remove—

I watch the man I love watch
the turn of the Sacramento River, then Sacramento,
lit city of legislation and flat land.

I think of Florida, how flat.
I think of forgetting Florida.
And then the landscape grows black.

Ode

Because this is California—
where moisture burns,
and birds pick at the Pacific's
thin waves with their beaks—
the neighborhood never noticed
the small blue-and-white house;

because of the summer crowds
at Ocean Beach, the dunes' graceful erosion,
the wheeze of wind and train,
we never gave a thought to that house,
paint chipped, resembling a fish camp
or a rural juke joint;

because cats the size of raccoons
slinked into gardens filled
with green tomatoes and cilantro,
the men who smoked outside
of the house never seemed threatening,
just tired, maybe a little drunk;

because the days were never silent,
and the state grew darker,
and the news stained our hands—
because the evenings began
so leisurely that tenants
sat by their windows

to watch the orange trash-barges
chuff past an orange sun,
who would have guessed, sipping
the last of his beer, that this
is a halfway house, and someone
will be murdered here tonight,

the prisoners' advocate, shot
four times in the face. The sun
crashes into the sea.

Night: A Fragment

He knows his body's in a rage, and yet
how nonchalant
disease, the end here
and not here, his schedule cleared.
Outside, the palms are stirred;

mosquitoes drone.
He doesn't want
the rash to spread:
he swallows pills;
the pills postpone.

But night will not relent,
the garish moon; the chills.
*I would just as soon we let
the living go on living*, James Wright said.
There's nothing left to be said.

Breakfast with Thom Gunn

in memory, 1929–2004

We choose a cheap hotel
because they're serving drinks.
We drink. I hear him tell
a tale or two: he thinks

that so-and-so's a sleaze;
and then there was the time
that Milosz phoned, oh *please*.
Another gin with lime?

I want to say that once,
I saw him dressed in leather,
leaning on a fence
inside a bar. Rather,

walking to the N,
I gush about his books;
he gives his change to men
who've lost their homes and looks:

how like him, I've been told.
Our day together done,
I hug him in the cold.
And then the train is gone.

Ovid in San Francisco

The ancient moon began to rise.
On Market Street, in fierce disguise,
the goddess Fama told me lies

about an older man who turns
to find his lover boy—then learns
the boy's been lost to one who earns

a seven-figure salary,
who owns an urban gallery
and counts his every calorie.

Another accidentally
exposed himself to HIV:
his dust became a cypress tree.

The muscle queen who's wearing red
to coax his husband into bed?
He'll end up getting burned, she said.

I promptly walked away before
she told a tale of guile or gore;
I stepped into Medea's store

in search of anti-aging cream.
Medea hummed "A Love Supreme"—
and in her eyes, a spiteful gleam.

Ganymede on Polk Street

I'm on a "date."
I bring his can
of beer: "I can
accommodate,"

I reassure
my ancient trick,
then grab my dick,
making sure

I seem obscene
enough. (I'm foul
but beautiful.)
Such is the scene:

beneath the god,
the polished leather
of his tether,
I whisper, "God";

he tries to spit
into my hair.
A boy for hire
must take this shit.

Orpheus at Café Flore

In this café, my boy, there's an art to not looking
as if you are looking

for a man. First off, you're wrong
to avert your eyes. Avoid the furtive. Long

slowly, your book a smart prop, your mug again
filled with warm milk. The night comes; it gets cold.

In the corner? Yes, here I am, an old,
flawlessly dressed god—my flesh grown thin—

taking my little pills, drinking
Earl Grey and thinking

of someone just like you, to fuck.
(And you of me, in turn? With luck.)

Modern Art

After seeing the satyrs in the Cadillac, I hailed
a cab: Gold's Gym, pretty please, and step
lively. So, can one still be a man and take step
classes? I grunt at the pec-deck; I am hailed

by the neckless as the queen
of a raunchy country. (It's a myth,
btw, the size of my Nikes.) Fuck myth:
give me a man, some hot ghastly queen,

any day—now. If I shave
my chest and my yes and my happiness,
will I find someone, some happiness?
Just as I start to peak, I'll shave

my head, instead (think *Full Metal Jacket*).
And throw on a cultish animal jacket.

To Francis Bacon

And then the man I loved, his beauty going fast,
looked past me, past you, past the shady
museum windows and some boy photographing his posed,
fashionable, now-thuggish posse; he looked to the past—

back to the BART train, a blue stain;
back to the glittering city, to a tender walk
through the Mission; back to the local
meth addicts, to the corner Socialist—

then further, to that dirty sleeper on 16th,
his cock flopped on the sidewalk
(and the double-back for a good hard look) . . .
Back to the charming carnage that is his life.

Stranded

at another holiday function—
the doilies wine-dark, the teeth
of our host perversely bleached—

I nibble a melancholy quiche Lorraine
and regard the televisions, plasma
and everywhere and always

replaying a loop from my beloved
stag film, *Lizard of One*.
A tipsy supermodel slurs,

beautifully, her bleak republic;
somewhere, a cat barks.
And who, who is that exquisite man

by the fire, stirring
a highball with his clauses?
It is Mark Strand.

It is still Mark Strand.

Reception

Our students, paid to cook,
drizzle yellow batter.
They manage not to look
at us as if we matter.

The table talkers switch
from code to crude to gun.
A colleague mutters, "Bitch."
Mascara starts to run.

Harmonicas like dust,
a fire like a saint—
and academic lust,
conventional as paint.

A ragged, tweedy cat
lies on the Murphy bed.
Goodbye to all of that,
the weak; the chic; the dead.

Career

A younger poet wrote to ask
an older for a blurb.
The older poet said Perhaps,
which meant Do Not Disturb.

But when the older poet saw
a photo of the lad,
the older man dipped his pen
and wrote that he'd be glad

to offer up the richest praise:
If Bishop wed Magritte,
these villanelles would be their spawn.
And maybe they should meet.

The younger poet cleaned his room.
He wore his tightest shirt:
when he fawned, he squeezed his arms,
his flex a sort of flirt.

They drank. The day went dark, then dead.
And love's the burning boy,
the older said, sliding a hand
up the comer's toy.

Postcard from California

Hart Crane, January 1928

The purling fountains, drawling mockingbirds.
The midnight shaking of geraniums.

Schoolmarms retired from Iowa along
with hobbling Methuselahs, alfalfa-fringed

and querulous, side by side with crowds
of unsuccessful strumpets of moviedom,

gorgeous to look at, and hordes of nondescripts
seemingly bound from nowhere into nothing.

The Long View

Two lovers sit atop
Dolores Park: they stop
their argument to see
a church, a bridge, a sea.

They play a little game:
each man proceeds to name
his list of lovers, dead.
There's no one left unsaid.

Anxious pigeons wait
for crumbs to fall. It's late.
The weather starts to shift:
all fog, all love, will lift.

N

has crawled out of the ocean
to carry us from sleep, like sleep,

the gray of outer Sunset portending
the gray of inner Sunset. And so on.

On the N, one should invent
intricate fictions for the lives

of the passengers: time is a game.
Soon we will be underground.

But first, the long lush green
of Duboce Park, the happiness of dogs!

Goodbye now to their owners
eyeing one another. Goodbye

to the park's locked men's room,
where once a man was found dead,

his penis shoved into his own mouth.
The world continues, the engine

of the world the letter N.

III

Let all flowers wither like a party.

— JOHN BERRYMAN, "DREAM SONG #32"

Ocean Beach

seems cruel this August,
the skeletal chill,
even the gulls a little
ambivalent. There are

warnings everywhere,
what passes for warning:
kelp like dead sea
creatures, ropy tails and flies;

the dog stalking the crow.
There's no getting around it,
either, the water, its epic
associations, etc.,

the foggy pull of the tide
toward the belated,
the false, the near tears. Beauty lies,
lies in unbeauty.

Translation

In the half-mist of Golden Gate Park,
new friends of friends, barely legal, swig
malt liquor, and I confuse The Shins
with Death Cab for Cutie (the kids snicker,
fiercely; I admire that). Cut grass

smells like sincerity: one Saturday,
long ago, my father, a suburban dream, sweaty
from yard work, took a call (his father, dying).
He sobbed, which unsettled, unsettles, me.
I am neither young nor old.

Lexington

There were horses in the field
on Harrisburg Road; and, further,
the adult theater. (*Look away*, Mother said.) After

the incidents at the sitter's house—
her son Jim; the *Hustler* in the basement;
a red scratch on my neck—

my sister and I were made *latchkey kids*.
And of course I loved the freedom:
crunching sugar cubes until it hurt; *Guiding Light*;

masturbating just out of sight
of my little sister. In the hours after
the indignities of elementary school, before

the return of the parents—that opening—
I started to feel something. It was contempt.

Design

A pile of white towels in the corner;
a duct-taped X on your bedroom floor.
The backdrop is pitiless, like a late Rothko,

the Marlboro smells belated—
and I grow nostalgic
for absolutely nothing. I want more than your little

lash marks, your vulgar watch. More
than art school. More than the greatcoat
in Tom Ford's last Gucci collection

(*I'm stunning*, the mirror lies). I want lust
as cold, precise, and prescriptive
as the en dash of a dead man.

The Rape of Ganymede

As Rembrandt saw it (the boy's posterior
bare, fleshier than a man's; the black air,
Macedonia's smoke; the rosy Trojan
all in a tizzy, his rags hitched up, urine
yellowing his left foot,
the jut of his white gut),
myth is a hoot. Look in the eagle's eyes:
he's lightly amused at the size
of the brat's fat hands, the fact of Ganymede's death-
grip on a pair of dangling cherries, both
of which are overripe—the eagle knows
the weight of thugs, of thunderbolts, of Eros.

Colloquy between A and B

A
That "girl" leaning on the bar
is no virgule—that's a real girl.

B
Say it like you mean it.

A
I mean: I long to say something
unsexed by breakage or mark.

B
Oh, you love them like you love
the ruthless participle,
the lying and the fucking.

A
Something full of breathing space,
the kind that discourages fire.

B
But the world needs its fire,
its cities of shame.

Intimacy

Because I live for beauty, which I hate,
I wipe the ants off my boyfriend's feet
at the bathhouse, where I lured him
in search of a third.

I like the low wattage here, the way
the steam obscures. In the rec room,
a naked man eats saltines
and nods the nod in our direction . . .

I want to leave this place
demeaned. It ought to leave a welt or rash.
Tonight, the corridors smell of bleach,
cherry air-freshener, and far too much

ambition.

Monday

While you wait for the J train, for work, think
of your new boyfriend, who loves apostrophes,
sizzle-pants, and you.
Who pointed out the "Andrew Lloyd Webber" house

and said his feelings have started to "Escalade."
You'll forgive him for now, smarty pants.
(Your last, the crisp progressive, declawed
his cat to save his Ethan Allen chairs.) Besides,

there's such promise, such furniture and new sex!
Look: wildflowers bloom in the streetcar tracks;
a syringe lies in the grass. It isn't
beautiful, of course, this life. It is.

Seeking

Because desire is treacherous, is
a starched crease in my Z. Cavariccis,

I'm seeking someone keen on hopscotch,
two fingers of Scotch

tape, and the words *Central Valley*. If you speak
to me lovingly, in your best porn-speak,

a night with me will be like a pop
quiz, or tart; like warm soda pop.

The night will throb like a shot at the free
clinic! I promise you, it won't be free.

Well, Here We Are

Doesn't it feel nice to get off
the digital grid? I like slow
jams, and piss and vinegar;

I like to mix it up, it's true. For you,
I recommend the zero option
(it comes with a free typewriter);

I'll have the entire pupu platter.
Like a frat boy, I enjoy hazing/
fundraising. And my hair is amazing.

For afters, let's make a worst-of list!
Old stick, let's make it last forever.

A View

Your look

is like a fashionable book:

white space, the meaning

all droll footnote in nine-point.

Life lengthens—

I could list the colors, but I'm no dead

philosopher. *Whatev*, you say,

not even bothering to end

your dismissal. Fine. I say

hush and scrutinize the sea: my linguist,

my one true bright hissing love.

South City

Even the pines are industrial-park green.
Blue is the tarp, blue the crane,
blue the siding of Building 6—
its smoke, the incinerated animals
of our biotech firm, commingles
with low clouds. (This city, like water,
waits for the end of industry.)
Now a jet, so quiet, jets past my cool
office window, past tall ships in the bay,
their masts like matchsticks—
but burned, already burned.
And the pier, like a lean prehistoric monster,
has walked, headfirst, into the sea.

Poetry

The flowers are all in a panicle,
and Eos goes on and on about
the lingering sea-stink. *Most good things
end up grilled*, some philosopher is said

to have said. The garden's not unfamiliar,
so grab a blade and dig in, eternally—
or at least for a few hours. Spring seems so inadequate:
but don't get frippery with me, not here.

Off in the trees—that's high silviculture.
The slug in the yard has its desired effect;
love becomes a fritillary. Lucky thing we bought a day-pass
before everything went doolally . . .

Fiction

For years, there was no hope. We had grown up
believing that the dead, while dead,
might stay awhile. That was not the first time
we were dead wrong. Strangers grew
more fictive than true. O there were muscles
and lunches and circuit girls, too! What a mess.

Wine coolers fell out of fashion, and flannel;
fuck-me pumps made a comeback. Come back,
dead soldiers, piled up by the bar
in the era of fresh flowers arranged
by the dead, a florist—what else? I'll tell you.
But soft, the story starts anew.

Notes

"The Mortician in San Francisco": This poem is for Tom Halloran.

"The Sunset": The Sunset is a district in San Francisco.

"Little Colonial Song": A few of the details are taken from William Bartram's *Travels*.

"Night: A Fragment": The poem quotes James Wright's "Northern Pike."

"Breakfast with Thom Gunn": The N is the N-Judah streetcar/metro line in San Francisco.

"Ganymede on Polk Street": Polk is a street in San Francisco, infamous for its male prostitutes.

"Postcard from California": Many details are indebted to Hart Crane's January 31, 1928, letter to Peggy and Malcolm Cowley.

www.ingramcontent.com/pod-product-compliance
Lightning Source LLC
Chambersburg PA
CBHW050911300426
44111CB00010B/1478